ANCHOR BOOKS

At Creation's Hand

Edited by

Steve Twelvetree

First published in Great Britain in 2000 by
ANCHOR BOOKS
Remus House,
Coltsfoot Drive,
Woodston,
Peterborough, PE2 9JX
Telephone (01733) 898102

HB ISBN 1 85930 753 1
SB ISBN 1 85930 758 2

FOREWORD

Anchor Books is a small press, established in 1992, with the aim of promoting readable poetry to as wide an audience as possible.

We hope to establish an outlet for writers of poetry who may have struggled to see their work in print.

The poems presented here have been selected from many entries. Editing proved to be a difficult task and as the Editor, the final selection was mine.

I trust this selection will delight and please the authors and all those who enjoy reading poetry.

Steve Twelvetree
Editor

CONTENTS

Choking

I choke on the bitter bland air,
which slowly starves my soul,
I can't breathe this tasteless fate,
I long for change, I sit, I wait.

But as I sit the trees corrode,
even the purest milk curdles,
corruption thrives consuming the weak,
no-one can see the God they seek.

Unity has withered and now is dead,
the foreboding future comes to head,
where to run? Nowhere to hide,
the doors of Hell are open wide.

Amy Cox (16)

Requiem

The trees on the hillside are cowering in terror,
Boughs semaphoring a prayer to their God,
While furious storm winds tear at their branches,
Beating and flailing them, sparing no rod.
Howling in triumph at each fresh torn twig fall,
Outshouting each anxious creak of despair,
Their final achievement, the great cataclysm,
Is welcomed with thunder and fire in the air
As the oldest and greatest centurion beech
Groans and surrenders, roots torn from the ground.
The battle is over: the wind is the victor,
Sorrow and triumph forever are bound.

Hark now in the hush
Of that moment of death:
All is airless and soundless -
An intake of breath -
And there in the wind-pause the host of the vanquished,
The undergrowth army of brambles and thorns,
Whispers of pain,
Bends earthward and mourns.

And, at last, in that tumult
Of fury and fear
The cotton wool night sky
Marks the death with a tear.

Ted Harriott

MOTHER EARTH

Grey clouds cover your horizons,
Dust falls to you the flexing host,
Blue, you move the golden grains of sand,
Green, you blend the unwanted with the lost.

Black as the Abyss of man's dreams,
Light shimmering surface covering coral,
Carrying warmth, and life, the breeze,
Mother of all and placed in peril.

Shape and movement, windborne laughter,
Gather fishermen and memory's tear,
Renewed, reshaped and cleansed forever,
Wind and tide and Earth join here.

R J Paget

A Fairy Tale

You won't believe this but it's true,
I saw a fairy - plain as you,
With dainty slippers and a gown
Of gossamer and softest down.
Bright silver glittered in her hair
Of tumbling tresses flowing fair.
She waved her wand that I might see
The magic she could weave for me.
I glimpsed again my long lost youth
And gazed on innocence and truth.
I watched a babe, unspoilt and pure
Grow sullied as it came mature
Then realised how, deep within,
With age we oft succumb to sin.
The fairy helped me then to see
How good a person I could be
If I would change my maverick ways
And shun temptation all my days.
So, that is why you see me pray -
Because a fairy came my way.

Vivienne Joyce

GENUS PLASTICUS

The genus plasticus
Is a fast growing breed
Long on their lifetime
But short on their seed
They multiply greatly
Like a common old weed
Thrive on the discards
That we no longer need

Plasticus Parakeetus
In great Windsor Park
Plasticus Binlinerus
A modern day lark
Marcus Donaldus
All make their mark
Growing profusely
By day and by dark

Plasticus Detritus
Cover the streets
Baggo Bassettium
Whose ova are sweets
And the common Wrigleyia
Whose droppings defeat
The efforts of townsman
And stick to his feet

The Plasticus thrives
In so many forms
Replacing the breeds that
In old times were norms
In sunshine and rain
And wild thunderstorms
They live in their millions
In hedgerows and lawns

Ray Ryan

OUR PLANET

This Earth of ours is a terrible place
War and violence hatred and waste
We should get together try to love and care
Give each other and want to share

See first to other people's troubles and needs
Regardless of colour country or creed
What happened to the feelings people call love
Maybe we should try asking our Lord up above

We seem to all have drifted too far away
Why have we left God's path and gone astray
If not in God then believe in each other
Try once again to be like sister and brother

This Earth of ours could be a beautiful land
If people would only learn to walk hand in hand
Get together at the start and end of every day
And for all our sakes find a better way.

Elizabeth Hollows

The Opposite Sex

The time has come to show the light,
Expose our plight . . . win the fight.
From Adam and Eve to millennium eve, and
Geri Spice on reaching new heights
One thing has not changed.
Men!

Stone age to 'New' age . . . give us a break!
They think it's just a piece of cake
And expect life ready on a plate.

We hear your cries of protest
Against the way we analyse, criticise and constantly test
The way we change the way you are
The way we prevent you going far,
aahhhh.

From talking Man U
To chomping your stew
From eyeing up chicks
To cheap pathetic kicks
From talking to your mates
and paying the pub's rates
you still ain't got a clue.

So to avoid moves to antagonise, let's reach a compromise
Let's make the effort, to avoid the sexist's rut.
To minimise the range, we both have to change!

Monica Aggarwal

Oh So Human

Lock 'em up, lock 'em down, keep the beasts
Hanging around. Here to please you, here to
Dance, to make the watchful eye so tense.

Such a wild existence. Captured from their home,
Now caged, controlled, obeying commands, not
Free to roam. This price you pay is no way to live
Out life, with no reason or motive. They are the
Master and the taker, it's all just a money-maker.

Innocence in anger, reflects the stronger, the mind's
Avenue is longer, than the holder of the key.

They say 'Release me. I was here before you, before
The first two. I was master of my kingdom. Now a
Slave I misbehave - the mirror image of seldom.'

They beat me and hate me, my state of mind and body
Isn't what it should be.

Solitude lengthens the barrier, around my entire,
Soldier-like existence.

Elliott Nash

THE WALL

The wall out-front is really great,
Built by Eddie and his mate,
They worked real hard to get it done,
I'm sure it could not have been much fun,
It runs along straight and true,
With bricks of red and some of blue,
I know that it will last forever,
No matter what the wind and weather,
So my thanks to Eddie and his mate,
I think your wall is really great.

Margaret Yardley

At Peace With The World

I have had my fill of death and hate
No more the seas will I roam,
The smell of cordite has vanished for good
And now it's the smell of home.

A home that is secure from the threat
Of a madman incensed with hate,
Who cost us tears, and blood and sweat
But the end was well worth the wait.

Admittedly the price was high
Our friends buried far and wide,
We can only honour their memory
And remember, for what they had died.

So now it's peace and all hands to the wheel
And let's get on with the task,
Of creating a world that's fit for us all
I think, that is all they would ask.

And then aspire to a world of equals
Marching forward, with flags unfurled,
Millions of loving families
Creating a better world.

So I've put away my guns and shells
And settled down in my chair,
With my loved ones thankfully by my side
Sans youth, sans teeth, sans hair . . .

Bernard Hallas

UNTITLED

Walking in the light of Jesus
Walking hand in hand with God
Singing praises Hal-Le-Lu-Jah
Jesus is our living Lord

Come and listen little children
To the stories oh so true
Jesus born in a manger
Born to die for me and you

Kneeling down beside my father
Kneeling down in silent prayer
Thanking Him for all His blessings
And His love and tender care

On the cross He hung and suffered
Bled and died to set us free
Then He rose in all His glory
He rose up triumphantly

When I hear the angels singing
When I see the peaceful dove
I will meet Him in His kingdom
Everlasting ever love.

Mary Turner

The Tortoise

Please God bless our tortoise
For he isn't very fast
When he's entered in a race
He always comes in last
I always feed him Esso
Which he doesn't like too well
For I've found out from experience
He runs easier on Shell.

I have a little tortoise
My mother calls him Fred
Last week I found him in the lounge
I thought that he was dead
I tried the kiss of life on him
And blew upon his beak
Then my mother told me
He won't awake until next week.

A E Gilbert

Rum And Readiness

Their eyelids droop and close
on the stockings hung at the ends of their beds,
whisperings fade away

Downstairs
the last parcel is wrapped
the last card written

She sits on the floor in front of the fire
bowl on her lap
creaming butter and dark sugar

Rum is added drop by drop
the mixture is tasted, found wanting:
so more rum, more tasting,

stirring, and
spoon to mouth
more liquor, a giggle or two

'You're sloshed' he says
'Mmmm . . . she says
in a befuddlement of rum and readiness.

Catherine Bradbury

What?

I've got a couple of cloth ears.
I'm a little bit Mutt and Jeff.
But though I may look vacant,
I'm not daft, just deaf.
And if your diction isn't good
I may not hear what you say,
For of all the words in my lexicon
The most used one is 'Eh?'
Looking around for my spectacles
I said to my wife one day
'Have you seen my glasses love?'
And I thought I heard her say
'They're in the bedroom,' so I went
Upstairs and looked around
But though I turned the room upside down
They were nowhere to be found.
Nor in the next room either
And, though for the past week,
I hadn't been in the small bedroom
I thought I'd take a peek.
But I drew a blank, so I called to my wife
'My glasses aren't up here,'
And her reply, roared in dulcet tones,
Floated up loud and clear.
'I said, they are on the breadbin!'
So I looked, and there they were.
When I put them on I could see what she said,
For though you may think it absurd,
If I've got my goggles on,
I can hear every word.

Peter Tickner

MANAGEMENT COURSE

Can't find a job? What a pity!
But there's no cause for tears or remorse.
Just forget disappointments and failures,
And sign up for our *'leadership* course.

The knowledge and skills that you offer
Will undoubtedly take you so far;
But your *assertiveness rating* needs boosting,
And your *self-esteem's* way under par.

Let us just get a grip on your *psyche,*
And give it our expert attention,
And you'll find that you're destined for much higher things,
Like a great big fat pay-cheque and pension.

Our *multi-disciplinary module*
Will provide what your life has been lacking,
And with it your shelf-filling job at the stores
Would have led to promotion - not sacking!

Our diploma in *Modern Stress Management*
Is the only degree you require.
Once we train you in *psycho-synthetics,*
You can have any job you desire!

Norman Ford

A Golden Bay (If Only It Was That Easy)

If only I cold fly away
To a light warm golden bay
Where life is simple free from pain
Laughter joy fun will keep you sane
Where each day you wake
Is a pleasure for your own sake.

To live be you - yourself alone
With never any reason to fret or moan
Where people are kind good and true
Never any reason to feel sad and blue
To give tender love to all you see
This cost nothing at all it's free
To think of others before yourself
You find and feel a different wealth.

Take me away to this far off place
And fill my spirit full of grace
I have no time for disarray
I know I now have plenty to say
With hurt, pain, despair, to mention a few
But hush say no more you already knew
Leave negative thoughts behind you for good
Turn round, look around, you know that you should.

Fix in your mind that beautiful place
You can go there for free no time to waste
With sea sand and the bluest of sky
It's all there for the taking in your mind's eye
For dreaming is free
Imagination is all you need to see
Remember the key
Let's go without delay, let's flee.

Susan Ponter

FRIENDSHIP

F riends are for having fun with
R eal friends stick by you no matter what
I nstead of breaking up with you
E ndless fun you may have
N ever ending your everlasting friendship
D eep inside you know you should
S tay friends until the bitter end
H iding and playing until the sun goes down
I nside each other's houses messing around and
P laying about. That's what friendship's all about.

Gabrielle Blakey (14)

That's Interesting

We were talking about football while we waited for the food.
Four of us - three lads and a girl.
Promotion, the World Cup and the merits
of three points for a win.

She just looked around as we talked, looking wistful and out of sorts.
So, I asked her, 'Do you want us to change the subject?
- You don't look that interested.'

'No, it's all right,' she said.
'I've got a season ticket for Blackburn Rovers.'

Simon Henry

The World

The world holds so many troubles
Life is fading, like the dying autumn colours
Where is the sanity, hate is breeding violently
People don't communicate, there's no way into heaven's gate
Good men have tried to carry on
But sexual thoughts turn evil on

Morale is changing, it's so frightening
Future life a hazy sighting
Greed, selfishness and vanity
Have swallowed peace and liberty
Nature's rainbow has faded down
By concrete blocks in every town
Children now are not being told what's black and white, what's hot and cold, they're not being told what path to take, what song to sing what love to make

It seems to me we're still going to ignore
Life's fine light and peace for evermore
But just you wait your time will come
We'll all regret what we've done
And realise that God's the one
To whom we all shall come.

Joanne Thomson

Words

Words revolving in my head.
Where they come from who can say.

From that great grey sludge of porridge
Can I lift new truth and knowledge?
Raise the cover see what's there,
Turn them gently while they're sleeping.
Watch them form and fade away.
This one, that one, now another,
New words, old words, very cold words,
Crowding, climbing, pushing,
Jostling hard for my attention,
Some from places I daren't mention.
Sorry words you none will fit.
Go back to sleep, while I sit
And cogitate that empty spot
For other choices from that pot.

Where are you hiding?
In which nook?
Come here word and let me look.
Do you mean just what you should?
Are you an impostor posing there?
Chosen just for sounding right.
If this goes on I'm up all night.

Then, one day when I'm not looking,
Just washing up, or maybe cooking,
The perfect word pops up, unbidden.
I'll never know where it was hidden.

Richard Neve

Self-Made Stylist

He never has a single care,
There's naught much can give him worry,
No matter what the time may be?
He never has a hurry.
Rises when it pleases him,
Does not retire till late,
The latest fashions don't trouble him,
But still he feels up-to-date.
He doesn't bother over-drinking,
The price of stocks and shares,
He never fears his business to fail,
He has no business to fear.
His face is always bright and cheery,
He very rarely beefs.
The reason why he is so happy,
He's still in nappies!

Ron Whitehead

NATIONAL SERVICE

They put me in the army to make a man of me
I swore to serve the Queen and defend democracy.
They asked me my religion - I said that I had none
It scandalised the chaplain - you should have seen the fun!
They sent me to the barber - he sat me in his chair
I told him, 'Just a trim' as he cut off all my hair.
They issued me with hobnails and marched me up and down
And when I did a pratfall the sarge called me a clown.
They sent me to the cookhouse to sample army food -
A plate o'wat'ry pom and a mug o'rosie, stewed.
I listened to a lecture delivered by a chap
Who championed the condom and warned against the clap.
They told me in the NAAFI, 'We serve no spirits here -
For officers it's whisky, for other ranks it's beer.'
They sent me to the doctor to have a shot or two -
He couldn't find the vein, no, he didn't have a clue.
The army fight instructor, he handed me a knife
And at his invitation I tried to take his life.
It took a tin o'Brasso to polish up my brass -
They had me bull my boots till the toe-caps shone like glass.
I lined up for inspection, I hung my head in shame -
The sergeant called me idle, the corp'ral took my name.
They handed me a rifle, they handed me a clip -
You should've seen 'em jump when I let the bastard rip!
They had me fix my bay'net and urged me to attack -
It demonstrates esprit to eviscerate a sack.

Robert John Orr

The Bulb

The bulb is planted in a pot,
Hardly showing like a dot,
With water, light they do regain,
To show their beauty down the lane.

Whether cultured or simply wild,
Their fragrance strong or mild,
They please us, oh so much,
Some we even don't dare to touch.

Some with beauty, some with grace,
Others decorate the space,
Once picked, they die away,
Never to brighten another day.

Some with poison, some with curves,
Some with extract of lovely herbs,
To take away some hurting pain
And once again our health to gain.

We feed, we treat in every case,
Our window bottoms there to lace,
With colours bright to see each day,
Would we have it any other way?

J Devine

DECEMBER SKY

Indigo blue slate grey
December sky.
Pacing slowly with tired tread
across the closing day.

Tree silhouettes in stark outline
against its massive canopy -
and weary fields closing their sun-drenched
cloaks around their furrows.
Looking back the way we have come
homeward bound, I pause by a stile
and offer quiet thanks.

Pamela J Rolinson

Perfection

He's not a bigot though he knows
He is the very best
And knows he's more intelligent
Than any of the rest.

He knows he's so good looking
It really is a shame
That there is no one like him
In feature or in fame.

He knows the country he should lead
If o'er its people he should reign
The world would be a perfect place
To him it's very plain.

Great wealth he would accumulate
People's respect he'd gain
And everyone would bow to him
As they followed on his train.

We all know he does not exist
Thank the Lord for that
But in each and every one of us
There's a bit that fits his hat.

So remember every morning
In your mirror what you see
Should be a mixture of your pride
And sincere humility.

Ian Russell

The Other Half

When the good Lord created the opposite sex
It was not quite in the way that a woman expects
Firstly a mother to cosset her son
To be there for the needs of this masterful one.

For when God made the female with compassion and care
He made it quite plain that for man she'd be there
To become his dear wife surely fills her with pride
His faithful companion to be by his side.

On her man she'll depend, handsome and strong
There to support her when things sometimes go wrong
A marriage of bliss, she stays loyal and true
Then dear little wife does what Mother would do.

She will iron his shirts and keep his home clean
Shows interest to know how his busy day's been
Dinner to cook and with the hand that is free
Settles him down with a nice cup of tea.

At 'do it yourself' he sometimes is hazy
His laid-back approach is driving her crazy
With a tap that is dripping, the leg off a chair
Says he'll do it one day when he has time to spare.

But the 'old-fashioned Eve' is never at loss
She cunningly tells him that he is the boss
Then emerged 'modern woman' sure-footed and glib
Something to do with the new woman's lib.

She sets out to her job at the break of each day
A reversal of roles, home her husband would stay
Poor baffled male, bemused and perplexed
But we love them, God bless them - The opposite sex.

Barbara Davies, Swansea

On My Celibacy

It really is a pity that babies are not brought
By storks nor found under gooseberry bushes.
Without fear of painful birth or risking to abort
I could, like Miriam, have found one in the rushes
Floating in a basket among the water lilies.
But a baby needs a father
As I needed a soulmate with compatibilities.
But where was this ideal suitor
Who had shared my previous lives?
Love is fleeting, fickle, finite.
There was no joy in being one of Henry's wives.
Divorce offers no delight.
Yet moonlight and roses of romantic novels can reflect life
As when eloping lovers plan a secret tryst.
From a first kiss to marital bliss, from bride to wife,
From courting couples to diamond weddings, some in accord co-exist.
But I a spinster will remain until my dying day
Bestowing my maternal affection on the friends
Of St Francis, birds, donkeys, fish and kittens at play,
Every creature who on our compassion depends.

Vivienne Brocklehurst

THE OPPOSITE SEX

I like men
I think they're great
In fact I think
They're
The perfect mate.
For woman of course.
Don't get me wrong
Don't pick the first one that comes along.
There are short and tall
Fat and thin
And then there are some
Who've got everything.
Of course I know some have got their faults,
But they seem to know all
About nuts and bolts.
On football they are all quite keen
And watch sport all day on the TV screen.
But who do you think always makes the tea?
Well yes you've guessed it
It's always me!

Olwen Counsell

MEN

Men can be so infuriating,
They think they know it all,
With cups of tea on the hour,
With wives at their beck and call.

Glued in front of the TV set
Remote control in hand
Up goes his hand as he changes channels
You'd think he was conducting a band.

But there is a softer side
As with his children he plays
On the day they were born he had
A grin that lasted for days and days.

Throughout their school and young adult life
He was at their beck and call
'Dad! Can you take me to dancing?'
'Dad! Can you take me to football?'

Yes! Men can be very annoying
I realised that from my wedding day
But I wish he was still like it now
You see, through death he's no longer with us today.

Yvonne Lewis

I BELIEVE IN

I believe in myself, almighty me
As I am great, there can only
Be one me, no one can be me
But me.

I believe in love, or without love
There is only hate and lust,
For love is a part of life.

I believe in money, for money is
Life, without money there shall
Be no life.

I believe in God, almighty God
For he is the creator of heaven
And earth and all human beings
And all little things.

I believe in my mother, for she's a jolly
Good fellow, for she is my creator, for she is
A saint and my guardian angel and
I love her dearly.

Dennis Rookes (15)

Life?

Can I write my feelings cold,
straight on paper, words so bold?
Is there any other way,
to tell the world,
I'm here, look, hey!

The past imprisoned in my breast,
if I can write, will I then rest?
Pleasure, pains, joys and grief,
these childhood memories find relief?

My soul a tortured butterfly,
seeks flower from flower, until it die.
Unsure of even right from wrong
the meek inherit, but winning's strong.

So I plod on, yet one more day,
I hope something will show the way.
That reason for eternal strife,
the future meaning of my life?

M A Spencer

For Her

Tomorrow
Tomorrow
There will be
A wall of silence
Between you and me
And wind will sigh
Gathering autumnal leaves
Under the wall of distance.

Tomorrow
There will be skies
Of distant thunders
And divisions of space
Will spill over
Colouring the seasons yellow
Tomorrow
There will be
Twilight of
Blood of vermilion
Or like the liquid
In the jilted veins.

Tomorrow
The blades of grass
Will stand like arrows
And their sharpness
Will cut asunder
The abruptness of immediacy.

Then the past will overwhelm
The unguarded present
Tomorrow there will be skies of distant thunders
Over the walls of silence and all the mutual blunders.

Durlabh Singh

Men! And Women!

Apart from physical differences
Much the same as women
Though women, so I'm told
Are hindered when swimmin'!
Both like to put others
In their place
Becoming commoner
Make-up, on a man's face
Cross-dressing, trouser suits
Ladies, in workmen's boots
Without their gel, on their head
Some men, wouldn't be seen dead!
I'm a man, who's fed up with hearing
Women complaining, about men leering
Can't they see, it's a compliment?
That an ignorant man
Thinks they're heaven-sent
Don't they realise
The power they hold
Simply by being
Brassy and bold?

Danny Coleman

Rough Trade

Give me a rough diamond
You can keep the old school tie,
Stiff upper lip, limp handshake
Play the game, do or die.

The public schools churn them out
So unprepared for life
Hell bent on acquiring 'possessions'
House, BMW, wife.

Brought up on 'it's who you know,
Not what you know' that matters
They bluff and double bluff
Till their frail ego shatters.

Then they have a mid-life crisis
(rehearsed for since they were ten)
And after expensive analysis
They can bluff and bullshit again.

Give me a man with no side
Not a poser or a sham
No politicians or ad-men
Just give me a real man.

Life isn't an easy ride
And when the going gets tough
I hope that by my side
There stands a bit of rough.

Kate Kerrigan

FAREWELL

'Farewell,' she whispered in my ear,
'I shall return within the year'
We vowed our love would still remain
And though the parting caused me pain
I felt no need to shed a tear.

While apart we still felt near,
Our letters bringing mutual cheer.
To any thought that love might wane -
Farewell.

Then I had a sense of fear,
The reason was at first unclear.
But then it all became quite plain,
She'd found herself another swain!
'And so, reluctantly, my dear -
Farewell.'

Frank Jensen

WHAT'S ALL THE FUSS ABOUT?

What is a man?
What is a woman?
It's the old story isn't it,
Who is the superior?
Who is the strongest?
Who is the more intelligent?
Who drives the best?
Well I'm a woman,
I say a woman is the better driver
Women are more intelligent,
Some men are stronger
Oh yes but some women are stronger than man
So what's all the fuss about?
We are all part of the human race
We must all get along
Men and women must live together in peace and harmony
I have a man
He's OK, I love him
He has me, I'm a woman
He loves me
So what's all the fuss about?

Michelle Knight

Ego Man (But You're Different)

For behold the caveman cometh
And the cavewoman wanted him to
For in swinging his club
While pursuing his grub
Unwanted intruders he slew

Conversation wasn't abounding -
He didn't gaze into her eyes -
But if pressed
He would talk just a little
Of his club -
Its weight and its size.

Now clubs have gone out of fashion
And the car has taken their place
Watch him wield his new toy with aggression
Hear it roar, hear it screech
See it race.

If it isn't the car, it's achievement
Or power, or money to burn
Or the birds that he'd bedded not wedded
Or the fact that
He's stony and stern.

And his skills of communication
Are set at about the same stage
For the cavemen who cometh
Remaineth
Different cave, different club, different age.

Dilly Parker

As One With You

I want to take you tenderly
enfolded within these protective arms.
As sheltered from the storms of life
while I purge away - all its harms.
Shrouded only in purest honesty
no use for lies or besmudging charms.

To caress your aching limbs
from all their encroaching dread.
While refreshing emotions suppressed
bringing nature's choice to head.
And be as one with you
proving all is true - as said.

A special - enchanted world
created there as just for you.
Where all that's wished becomes reality
and each moment's cherished true.
With sparkling skies of maraudic turquoise
spent always - being as one with you.

Gary Finlay

The Opposite Sex

Why do men have to be so macho?
See a woman in a car and they have to pass you.
They're good for some things true enough.
Gardening, fixing plugs, mending cars and all that stuff.
But why do they have to be so macho?

They jog about and go to the gym.
All of this to feed their ego.
Why can't men be more like us?
Gentle and tender not so volatile.
We women are caring not so hostile.
Why do men have to be so macho?

But where would we be without them I say?
We need their help to procreate.
To stop us being like a broody hen.
To give us a kiss, hold our hand
And give us a hug now and then.

Can we live without them?
No sirree!
Macho or not they're good enough for me.

Anne Shipley

Two Of Us

He says he's stronger lifting things
This maybe possibly true
But he moans twice as much
When he's caught the flu!

He says he can manage money well
And keeps it safe and hid
But when it comes to paying bills
He's never got a quid!

He says he's the one who's always right
Can never be mistaken
So why do I keep mopping up
For us to see daylight?

He says he's happy as can be
For me to eat sweet things
He can't do this anymore himself
And when I do, he hardly sings!

He says he's brave as brave can be
Would protect me against all war
But if he thinks trouble's lurking
He sends me to the door.

He gives me gifts, just what I need
And smiles as each one's opened
He forgets I got them for myself
As I know, never would he do the deed.

For all of this, he's loyal true
I liked him from the start
And if I'm honest straight and kind
I can't see us ever part.

Joan Richardson

VISITORS

We came to see the beauty, look
at nature, feel the breeze,
love each other, be so grateful
to the God upon the frieze.

Instead we caused this horror of a
world obsessed with hate,
each man killing his neighbour
and abandoning his mate.

Is the whole place going crazy
or was it meant to be a laboratory
for creatures rearranged in history,
supposed to stay all shrouded in
a vale of mystery.

Jean Paisley

NATURE'S FIREWORK PARTY

The big bang theory
Slowed down for observation,
Captured on film
By underwater cameras,
Like exploding stars
Millions of seeds are launched
And disperse throughout the ocean.

Nature's fireworks party
Candles, sparklers and rockets,
Burning wheels beneath the sea
Spinning wheels of colour
Blues and greens and reds
A painting on the seabed
Through the prism turns to white.

This image fires my imagination
I witness the beginning of creation
My mind goes bang
My thoughts are high like sky rockets
As life celebrates life
The wheels of creation are turning
Self-propagating fires are burning.

Nature's firework party
Normally unseen
Captured on film
That we are all blessed to see.

Ian Barton

Spirit Of The Hills

Beneath the backdrop of the Malvern Hills
Of ancient granite rock formation
Rising sheer out of the Severn Plain,
The rugged hills on my horizon
Stretching as far as the eye can see
Casting benevolent shadow below.

On foot traversing Malvern Wells Common,
Place of adventure and make-believe,
Last stretch of grassland at the hills' base,
Crossed the bridge over murmuring stream
Beginning life flowing on hillsides,
The splendour of the ridge looming nearer.

Following the lower path to St Anne's Well
Meandered through pinewoods, wide valleys,
Wandering through a web of foliage,
Tall trees quivering against the sky
Rustling like the skirt of a girl's dress,
Sun filtering through interlaced branches.

Fields stretched endlessly over Severn Vale,
Bredon Hill rose gently from the plain,
Beyond, merging with sky, Cotswold Hills.
Climbing to the highest point, westwards
Ridge after ridge, remote Welsh mountains
Beckoned again to their lonely terrain.

High on Malvern Hills brings deep contentment,
Place of inspiration and worship
Where mind can wander free from clamour,
In the silence of the steadfast hills
More reverent than any Cathedral,
There, a spirit of joy pervades the air.

Betty Mealand

Our Earth

One day we will know,
One day when it is too late.
Our planet will suffer,
With all the smoke
And all the fumes.
We will destroy our earth,
Forever it will be gone,
Gone for good.
It will be too late,
Too late to mend our ways.

Bo Blewis

THE FIELD

The crow stands forlornly
The skylark darts but does not bother to look.
The field only echoes the songs of workers
Labouring for a crust of bread
And a bowl of watered-down broth.
They were schooled in etiquette
In a time devoid of crime and addiction.
We have come to label work as work
When the product of work is respect.
A 100 horsepower tractor now runs guard
Against any unwanted invader be it flora or fauna
But there was a time when two honest horses
Ruled by earned respect.
Never did they have to show or prove their place,
Everything natural is being punished
As the machine scavenges over the bones
And sends the soil the colour of death
Consequence has been murdered
Redemption is blocked for we are
Weak through our own strength.

Jason Senior

Our Countryside

A Natural World I would love it, if only it could be,
The beauty of the countryside, for one and all to see.
All in its natural glory, nothing disturbed at all,
Majestic trees left growing, stately strong and tall.
Wildlife able to pick and choose where they would like to live,
Not roam into towns and cities, for the pittance that we may give
I'd like to see them fit and strong, let nature take its course,
Catch the prey they'd like to eat, which we would all endorse.
I wish they didn't have to fear - us humans - as they do,
A miracle it would be if they could trust when in danger, a few.
Come to us for protection, when wounded or filled with fear,
For us to love and care for them, until they get the *all clear*.
When we go for picnics, we are in *their* territory now,
There should be regulations, we should be made to vow.
Don't leave behind our litter, opened cans or broken glass,
The damage we could do to them, would maim or kill alas.
A worthwhile scheme to help them, stop the suffering, we will
Do something about it, accomplish and fulfil.
We should think before we just discard, things of no use anymore,
Polluting rivers and streams where they drink, we
have to be made to make sure,
Be more careful, treat the countryside with thoughtfulness and respect,
Then countryside, their territories, we could roam, be seen to protect.
If not it *will* all disappear, which would be quite a shame,
Don't want to see our wildlife, all docile quiet and tame.
Put in cages that's not natural, they'd be miserable and sad,
Wildlife in fenced-off places no freedom like they used to have.
No - let them have their habitats and havens for refuge,
Yes - to keeping a natural world, 'looked after' we've nothing to lose.
To keep our environment as scenes of beauty, not
factories, roads or brick walls,
Our countryside and scenic beauty, for nature, duty calls.

Beverley Diana Burcham

THE HANDS OF TIME

The thing about age
I hate and resent
Is the sight of my hands
So swollen and bent.
I can put up with wrinkles
And hair turning white
But the change in my hands
Is a terrible sight.
Once they were dainty
With nails pearly pink
I had to wear gloves
To wash up in the sink
Then, when I was young
And my hand's a disgrace
My mum never minded
When I patted her face
But now I can't knit
Or crochet, or sew
And when they are painful
I feel useless and low.
But I know I can't grumble
I've legs and can walk
And, counting my blessings,
Thank God, I can talk.

June Davies

Where Have All The Sparrows Gone?

Where have all the sparrows gone?
We don't see them no more
Where have all the sparrows gone?
What's happened to them all.

I used to go to the park
Every single day
To hear the sparrows singing
To watch the children play.

But now as I am sitting there
Silence fills the air
What's happened to the sparrows?
Why aren't there any there?

Alan Green

UNMAKING WOLVES

Before the white man made America
He unmade it. He unmade the forests,
Bison, native peoples, wolves, mountain lions;
Our genius is for unmaking. This
New world was a diamond with facets
Too bright, too boastful to be left alone
Their challenge was defiance, so they had
To be dismantled, like a bicycle.
The bits, not tumbled into drains or crushed
In the scramble, were cobbled up to be
Another of Mary Shelley's creatures.
When we have finished unmaking the world,
About next Tuesday - we can finish off
The only work left - unmaking ourselves.

Marianne Whitelaw

MIDNIGHT DREAM

Gold is the path to the setting sun
Alight on the ocean when day is done
While in the heavens the moon appears
Midst a million stars of a thousand years.
Gems of shells glint in soft sand
Silver sea caresses land
Rock pools pale with moonbeams' shine
Where emerald strands of seaweed twine.
Early frost does glisten shore
Pure delight from Nature's store.
Rippled grains with sparkling sheen
Oh perfect, perfect midnight dream . . .

Anita Richards

TREE OF LIFE

Brain, which shelters seeds, from which many
Mysteries arise.
Eyes, are the depth, of the flower
That grows.
Nose, is an ocean, of scent
That spreads.
Lips, seal the kiss of many worlds
Which it protects.
Neck, leads to the heaven's doors above all,
Which all respect.
Arms, which are my survival
Stretching, reaching, growing.
Legs, are my roots on which I stand,
A strong stand I shall.
I am the creation of God,
Which nobody has the right to
Destroy.
To survive, I shall fight, with my
Heart, body and soul,
Because God has
Given me life . . .

J K Bhatoy

The Environment's Unfriendly

The environment's unfriendly,
Because of acid rain.
It's falling quite relentlessly,
Upon the earth's terrain.

The environment's unfriendly
Because of toxic waste.
That flows down every waterway
It's an absolute disgrace.

The environment's unfriendly,
The seas are like a bin.
In which man empties everything
Not accepting it's a sin.

The environment's unfriendly,
Because much land's now dead.
Soon man will live in deserts
With no corn to grow for bread.

The environment's unfriendly,
Man will soon have had his day.
For unless he takes more interest
Mankind will soon be - clay.

J Blades

THIS IS OUR CHILDREN'S LAND

The polar ice caps are melting drop by drop
The great oceans are swelling and land is lost
Pollutions have thinned the ozone layer
Letting through the sun's most harmful rays.

Islands vanish beneath the waves
Rain forests diminish in great swathes
Creatures gone forever, never to return
Why oh why don't we all learn?

Many animal habitats are lost
Widely-used pesticides, insure our good crops
The food they need is poisoned through
Very soon it could be me and you.

Mother nature is angry and shows her wrath
Sending earthquakes and floods into our path
We must learn to treat her with respect
Or our children will have little left.

Recycle our waste to save our land
Our cars should more often in the garage stand
Take care of our creatures who live far and wide
And just maybe we can all survive.

Our earth is ill, the signs are there
But do enough of us really care?
Do we want our children to inherit this earth
While this generation just watched its hurt?

Christina Cox

The Natural World

Man oh man what have you done
To this wonderful planet beneath the sun?
You've been given all power to rule,
A brain to learn from Nature's school.

Man oh man what have you done?
The earth cries out beneath the sun.
Innocent creatures both great and small,
No longer trust, they flee and run.

You're robbing the birds, cutting down trees
No berries or leaves for birds and bees.
Minnows and fish that live in the seas
You are polluting and destroying me.

Dominion you've been given over us
You are not the one we can trust.
Polluting the air, destroying the place
What shall become of the human race?

Man oh man what have you done?
You destroyed our home beneath the sun.
Stop, remember, before it's too late
We reap what we sow . . . our fate!

Elizabeth Grant

KEY OPTIONS

Many decisions are made every day
Whether to accept, offer or turn down.
Trivial, vital, others' throwaway
Incorrect discernment may start countdown.

Impulsive reply in temper or haste
Could cause consequences haunting for years.
Igniting praise, perhaps leave aftertaste
From sparkling romance to severance tears.

Indecision tempts chances to blow cold,
Judgement pirouettes on estimation.
At crucial times essential to be bold,
Seeking certainty leads to stagnation.

Each key option unlocks different doors,
Access to another life evermore.

Hilary Jill Robson

Creation

Oh Lord (if such a thing there be!)
Why didst Thou make such misery?
When Thou hadst formed a world so fair
What madst Thou introduce despair?
What rich green pastures Thou hadst made
Which flocks could graze on, unafraid.
Had Thou not fashioned predators.
What madst Thou create carnivores?

Dissatisfied with monstrous hulks
With grotesque, grey reptilian hulks
That oozed through prehistoric slime
Didst Thou yearn for a sweeter time?
And didst Thou then long to replace
These monsters, with their lack of grace
With eagles, swans and humming birds;
With lions, lambs and deer in herds?

And when there dawned the fateful day,
Lord, didst Thou smile, or sadly say
'The world, according to My plan
Is ready now to welcome . . . Man?
Thou watched him rape the virgin soil
And plunder, pillage and despoil;
And whilst he played his wanton part,
Wast Thou resigned, or sick at heart?

For Thou raised no restraining hand.
Lord, could it be Thou *really* planned
Two million years of evolution
To be destroyed by our pollution?

Pauline Mackey

A Visit To The Hospital

Today was my day to be assessed
Got, I'm afraid, rather stressed.
Everyone there was very kind
and tried to give me peace of mind.
Told by the Doctor to sit and wait
hard not to get into a state!
Sandwiches and coffee were
supplied with a smile,
We were told we would have
to wait for a while.
Hope the Doctor is not too long.
When he *does* arrive . . .
I shall burst into song!

Pamela Butler

OCEAN LOVE

Your love is like the ocean
vast and gentle and serene.
Your eyes are glittering emerald seas:
The kisses of your lips
are like sweet whispering waves
washing over me.
Such joy to taste you
monarch of my dreams.
Yet you love with a violent passion,
crashing me against you
like a demon unleashed;
I am drowning in your arms,
you devour me;
unceasing, pitiless.
Together we ride the storm out.
We ebb and flow . . .
Ebb and flow,
until, finally we reach
a state of frenzied ecstasy
bursting forth unwavering passion
over sun-kissed sands.
Our souls are joined
smashed up against each other
in a melted, twisted heap;
We lie half dead and breathless
you and I . . .
Flotsam and jetsam
on the beach.

Denise Jones

THE JEWELLED CIRCLE

Trapped in a tangle of jewellery dross
It was lying in a cardboard box.
Its previous owner would have wept
To witness such gross neglect.

Reminiscent of a bygone age, where
Chivalrous knights met ladies fair,
The pendant lay on a long dark chain
Covered in decades of shame.

I knew that I must rescue it,
So I paid my fifty pence
And carried it hence with the greatest care,
Anticipating beauty there.

I set to work with liquid soap
And a gentle caress, in the hope
Of revealing the intricate silver, designed
With variant stones in a circle aligned.

The elegant chain now silver shone,
Its clasp showed old world aplomb.
It safely supported the circle so fine,
The pendant I cherished, now mine.

It aspires to the mystery of perfection
To be seen in the sun at dawn,
Symbolised by Giotto's O
In his circle drawn.

Market value matters not,
Intrinsically it's fine.
The craftsmanship is all in all
In a work of rare design.

Elizabeth Atkinson

Tranquil Dawn

If in the silence of this Sabbath dawn
My earthly life should cease,
Eternity will bring no greater joy
Than this stillness and peace.

And if I leave the birdsong and the dew
And lush green of the spring,
When all creation comes to life anew
And flowers are burgeoning,

I shall remember in that spirit-land
The sunshine warm and bright,
The scented breezes freshening the day
And stars decking the night.

Can heavenly realms be lovelier than this world,
Or angels be more fair?
Yes! There is One who makes that life supreme:
The Lord who reigneth there.

His presence will outshine the brightest sun,
His love will make us whole,
And his soft voice will welcome all who come,
With peace to every soul.

Constance M Driver

MAGILLYCUDDY REEKS

Up the breezy mountain, down the roaming glen
Gazing in wonderment at a pile of funny blocks,
Beside a cottage wall, whose thick thatched roof,
Gives a homely touch, peeping from the stony lane,
Surprise a song, 'Cockle-doodle-doo,'
Greets me before my hand has reached the door,
A loving moo, a distant baa, had the grey donkey a wink?
Funny feels populated, but where's the people?
'Good-day my dear, looking for the Missus?'
Cap raised above a grinning face, atop an Aran sweater,
Glimpsed o'er the pile of dark blocks.
A heavily-bunned woman pops smilingly out of the half door,
An auld pinny tied round her middle, big iron pot in her hand.
'Another bucket of turf my man, the fire needs stacking up,'
So that's the pile I wondered, did it house a pig!
As a friendly mongrel sniffed around me,
Birds trilling in the honeysuckled hedge, reflecting
Shining sun, 'Was ever home like this?' I gushed,
As I dipped my head beneath the wooden linteled door.
'Sure Ireland's a homely place, warm your feet by the fire,
And your heart with a wee Irish tot,
While the Missus tends to her good Irish stew.'
The cat purred contentedly under my stroking hand,
I just felt the same . . . *Content.*

Anne Mary McMullan

Pray For Them

Pray for the suffering and the harm
Pray for the mother with a baby on her arm
Pray for the grieving, pray for them so
Pray for the little ones who have nowhere to go
Pray for the hungry and deep despair
Who have lost their world and have no-one to care
Pray for the people who have lost hope
Let's pray together and pray for them to cope
Pray for the dying, pray for the weak
Pray for the old man whose outlook's very bleak
Pray for the starving who have lost hope
Let's pray together and pray for them to cope.

Amen

Julie Taylor

Measures Of Time

Sometimes I feel that I have lived forever.
Three or four lives strung together
And all important.

Then I consider 1000 years
A measure that I can't understand,
Can't count on my hand.

Did those who came ahead
And are now dead
Think *their* lives did it all?
Does it take Millennium to make me feel so small?

Jacquie Richardson

Chorus

I rejoice! In Christ's tradition
that life on earth, will bring the Lord's vision,
when living by God's commandments, is my decision,
mindful! That birth to death, is the mission,
The key to Heaven's door, my life's ambition.

Stephen Peden

A Chair

Here I sit, made of wood looking good
Hard, soft long and strong
Short wide narrow with pride
For you to rest your tired legs
And enjoy the view I'm giving you

I'll make you comfy, wait and see
You'll come back to sit on me

I'm getting old and getting bold
I can tell you stories I've been told

But first you have to have a seat
Keep me company and keep me neat.

Jim Ferguson

I Wish I Had . . .

As I grow older, I recall,
I wanted nothing old at all.
My Granny's 'Wotnot' filled with Goss,
I gave away, Oh! What a loss!
I see balloon-backed wooden chairs,
They cost so much at Antique Fairs.

The claw-foot bath so wide and deep,
I swapped for coloured plastic - cheap!
I wish I had them here today,
Those keepsakes that I gave away.
It isn't till these things have gone,
We realise what we should have done.
We should have saved them - held them fast,
The memories of a childhood past . . .

Margaret W Farrand

IT'S AUTUMN

The morning sun, the gentle breeze,
disturbing mounds of fallen leaves.
With hues of russet, brown and green,
the trees majestic, stand supreme.

It's autumn:

The sheep still grazing in the field,
'side neighbouring ones with harvest yield.
Strutting pheasants, the males who preen
unconcerned at being seen.

It's autumn:

In the garden, the robin's song,
reminding us that summer's gone.
From door lintels, like dewy lace
the spiders' webs fall on the face.

It's autumn:

In this the season that we love,
we count our blessings from above.
Sights and sounds and scented air,
it's wonderful, beyond compare.

It's autumn:

Margaret Bell

Self-Destruction

A thousand years and here we stand
Convinced of our divinity
And self-destruction's well in hand

Wreaking havoc on the land
Pollution of the air and sea
A thousand years and here we stand

Wars each century has planned
With prime use of technology
And self-destruction's well in hand

Spacecraft search for worlds, unmanned
They hurtle through the galaxy
A thousand years and here we stand

Global warming takes command
Gives orders for catastrophe
And self-destruction's well in hand

Ignorance that we expand
(Our one reliability)
A thousand years and here we stand
And self-destruction's well in hand

Kim Montia

IS ANYBODY LISTENING?

Why doesn't someone love me, what
have I done wrong?
Do I have to go on hurting, why
can't I belong?
I see other children happy, why
can't that be me?
Won't somebody listen, please help
me to see?
I try hard to be quiet, and not
make any noise.
Is the same thing happening, to
other girls and boys?

Is anybody listening, can anybody
hear?
I'll try not to tremble, whenever you
come near.
Won't somebody help me, can't you
hear my plea?
What's it like to have a cuddle,
no-one cuddles me!
What's it like to have a story,
to be tucked up safe at night
Knowing someone's there, if you wake
up with a fright.

Won't somebody tell me, what it
is I'm doing wrong?
Won't somebody love me, to show
me I belong?
I am one of many, I don't
know what to do!
I need someone to help me, is
that someone you?

Mary Brown

OVERWHELMING SURPRISE!

80 years young today!
I must thank God and pray.
Cards and presents I received
So many, I could not believe!

To think I have so many friends
Congratulating me
Making me so happy.

My family too -
Gave me such a surprise.
My husband and I had to be ready
For 7 o'clock, a knock at the door
There a chauffeur escorted us
Into a white Rolls Royce.
Oh! What a surprise! We looked at each other
Wondering where we were going
'I have to take you a scenic route
But mustn't say where!'

To our amazement, we arrived
at *Belvoir Castle.*
Where our family from far and wide
waited to greet us.
I was overwhelmed with joy
as only Carol and my family
knew what delight this would give me.
Cocktails and dinner too at Belvoir Castle.
How I thank God for a family so true.
For the love of a family's like no other
To show such love for a Mother.

G Davenport

NAN

How many years has she been a Mum?
Thinking that her work was done.
She quietly crept away to rest
Knowing she had done her best.

But not for long her peace would last
She knew for sure her time had passed
When welcome voices shout and scream
And drag her from her quiet dream.

'Nan oh Nan! Please are you there?'
Am I the answer to their prayer?
Do they know how much I pine
That the prayer they answered
was mine . . .

A Stubbs

Disappointment At The Gates

Sorry, but I don't know you . . .

Of course you know me Lord, I was at your church each Sunday
Okay, I was like many others, I'd forgotten it all by Monday.

But I read my Bible every day, well most days, but that wasn't bad
And I prayed for just about everyone whether they were happy or sad.

I took my marriage vows seriously, other women didn't enter my mind
I gave lots of money to charity, in fact I thought I was kind!

I went to Bible Class and helped at BB, I even helped stack up
the chairs
I did my share of repair work and helped at the Christmas Fayres.

I didn't tell lies, well maybe the odd one. I didn't drink or gamble
or swear
You certainly didn't hear me blaspheme and for others I really
did care.

So Lord, you surely must know me, I feel like a Christian alright
So why can't I come into Heaven, I believed in Him on your right.

. . . . . .

I'll tell you my son why you're not coming in, the reason is simple
and plain
You did good things in your lifetime, but you just weren't
Born Again.

All that you did simply wasn't enough to get you through the gates
So turn around and head down below to join a lot of your mates.

You didn't give your life to me, you didn't repent of your sin
You only pretended to be Christian so that's why you're not coming in.

All you had to do on earth was to bring me into your heart
Then, from that very moment your Christian life would start.

But no, you chose the easy way out, it would have been tough, that's true
But my Will would have guided your life so that's why I don't know you!

Maurice Langley

THIRTY PIECES OF SILVER

For thirty pieces of silver
Judas betrayed His Master
Peter a favourite disciple denied Jesus thrice,
declaring and swearing
he never knew the Master.

Jesus the meek shepherd of the sheep
betrayed again by Judas,
With a mocking kiss on the cheek.
The scoffing sign for Roman soldiers
to take hold of Jesus.
Leading Him away to be crucified
on the cross at Calvary.
Judas ran into the temple
filled with shame and despair.
Throwing the thirty pieces of silver
on the temple floor
When he found no one did care.
Judas who betrayed the Son of the living God
could live with himself no more.
He sealed his awful doom
going out the temple door
thirty pieces of silver lay scattered
on the temple floor.
Judas went out and hanged himself
his guilt he could stand no more.
Jesus was denied, betrayed, crucified,
The price He paid, His blood was shed,
at a place called Calvary.
We are bought at a price . . .
The price of Jesus' precious blood.

Francis Gibson

God's Acre

Tread softly, tread softly upon the green sod,
Remember, remember the Acre of God.
Here lie the bold, the bad and the good,
Asleep in their narrow hard pallets of wood.

There's somebody's mother and somebody's wife,
Taking the rest she deserved all her life.
Somebody's father and somebody's son,
For them, still the drumbeat, the crack of the gun.

There's somebody's sister and somebody's friend,
The Lord held a council and bade them attend.
And 'neath the white stone with an angel above,
Lies somebody's sweetheart and somebody's love.

Tread softy, tread softly upon the green sod,
Remember, remember the Acre of God.
Here lie the bold, the bad and the good,
Asleep in their narrow hard pallets of wood.

Sheila St Clair

A Special Visitor

Granny was in my room last night
I felt her presence there.
She must have known my worries
She thought that we should share
The thoughts in my head
Just going round and round.
God must have known my worries too
Because he sent Granny down.
We talked and talked for ages
And talked my problems through.
She helped me with my worries
She told me what to do.
I thanked her for her kindness
Said I missed her well and true
She leant over and kissed me
And said she missed me too.
And all at once she vanished
I was all alone . . .
I smiled to myself and thought
God must have called her Home.
I know she'll always help me
She'll always be near.
She'll know my thoughts, hear my words
And come back to calm my fears.

Laura Smith

JANUARY

Frost-spangled starry nights,
Cold days, the pale sun gleaming
And sweet, dark mysteries
In the long night stirring.

White breath on frosty air,
The young children playing
Warmly clad, with shining eyes
Their bright faces glowing.

Dark footsteps on white snow
Dark branches swaying
Pale light from cottage windows
Stars across the night sky moving.

M J Fisher

My Nose

My eyes looked down,
What's this I see?
Nothing but you, looking at me!
I tried to shake you off my face,
I tied you up with my shoelace.
But all you did was stick so fast,
Were you a monster from my past?
I stared at you and with a frown,
Hoped you would just fall right down;
Onto the ground and rush away,
But all you want to do is stay;
Upon my face, what shall I do?
I'd cross my eyes but then there's two!
I just won't look at my feet,
Or the stones on the street.
I'll keep my head straight and tall,
Then I won't see you at all!

Rebecca May Lister

THE FESTIVE SEASON

It's Christmas Eve, a festive time,
Mince pies to eat with hot mulled wine.
A Christmas Tree, ablaze with lights,
Brightening a cold dark night.
Holly, bright with berries hung,
Carols by the choir sung.
Christmas cards from folk you know,
An open fire with warming glow.
Parcels wrapped with loving care,
Food prepared for friends to share
Stockings hung at end of bed,
Small ears alert for Santa's tread.
Mother getting in a flap,
Has she done this, has she done that!
Hoping everything's complete,
It's up to bed, perchance to sleep.
Enjoy each moment Christmas Day,
For time so quickly slips away.

Dinah Court

The Teacher

When I'm tucked up within my bed
and I've laid down my sleepy head
Before I drift away to sleep
I wonder why the goats and sheep
have woolly coats and don't eat meat
and why the songs of birds are sweet
And why the moon comes out at night
and the sun by day gives such delight
And does the tide go back and forth
because it goes from south to north
The gardens with their pretty flowers
grow lovelier after sun and showers
When I grow up I'll take a book
the answers will be there when I look
I'll read and learn and try to remember
the days and dates from January to December
The information is there for us all
for you and me whether big or small
But now I must away to dream
so that I'll be bright and in the stream
where clever people who like me
will go to University
And then my knowledge I will share
when I sit on my teacher's chair

A Tompkins

Sleepyhead

My cat is such a sleepyhead
He always insists on going to bed
I wonder if he ever dreams
Because he shakes (or so it seems)
I used to think
He dreamt of things
Like . . . falling off a bike
Perhaps he got stuck up a tree?

I don't know . . .
        So don't
                ask
                    me!

Kim Blank

BEDTIME

'TV off! It's time for sleep.
Those hands need scrubbing
and brush those teeth.

I know you're tired but
it's got to be done;
Remember . . . washing can be fun!

The sink's too full it will overflow!
Act your age . . . you're almost four!

Please not too much splashing
I've just cleaned it all
Why is there toothpaste on the wall?

I'm losing my temper and I don't like to
but *why* must you do the things you do?

Now . . . that is better, all bright and clean.
Warm PJ's on - sorry I was mean.
It's been a long day for us all,
watch those toys . . . or you'll fall.
Now into bed, will you read to me?
And then my turn, which book shall it be?

That was a nice end to the day,
now close those eyes, no more questions today.
My lovely little boy so quickly you grow,
I may scream and shout - but I love you so.'

xxxxx

Irene Davison

Bedtime

I don't want to go to bed
in that bedroom on my own.
It's full of ghosts and ghoulies
and they know that I'm alone.
My toys all look like monsters
I think they're watching me.
If I close my eyes they'll go away
One, two, three.
I can see again
but they are still there.
A clown, a dragon, an Action Man and a teddy bear
they normally are my friends.
I take them to the park
but they all look so different
up here in the dark.
Mummy and Daddy say I'm silly
and shouldn't be so scared.
It's easy for them to tell me that
they go to bed *in pairs!*

J M Smith

On A Summer's Day

On a summer's day
The hills abound
With the sound
Of children at play

Excitement in their voices
Happiness that they feel
Wondering what new adventure
Their journey will reveal

The wonder of the mystic places
That lures them far away
From cobbled streets
That surround their home
Satisfying their wanderlust
And their need to roam

O'er pastures green they frolic
As cattle idly lie
On a carpet of clover
'Neath a clear blue sky
As the plover hides away
On this summer's day.

James Nicol

Best Friends

My best friend's called Harry
He's with me every day.
He stays by me when I sleep
He runs with me when I play.
He never ever leaves me
He doesn't ever roam.
He's at my side constantly
Outside or in my home.
Harry loves to run and play
He makes me laugh, he makes my day.
We roll around and play in mud
We hide behind trees down in the wood.
We swim, play ball and other games
We just call him Harry. He has no other names.
He's big and so strong, just like me
So why can't Harry climb the tree?
Mummy shouts. It's time for tea
A big bone for Harry, baked beans for me.
Good dog Harry, time for bed
He climbs in his basket, lays down his head.
I watch some tele then off upstairs
And guess who sits by me
When I say my prayers?
. . . *Harry!*

Sylvia Wood

SUNDAY SCHOOL

There's a picture I carry around in my mind
of a man - who was both gentle and kind.
But people didn't listen to what He'd say
and they set about to crucify Him one day.

He gave up his life so willingly
so that we could live in harmony.
He did not ask for riches or fame
but just to be loved . . .
Jesus was His name.

R Leddington

Perfection Personified

How
I simply adore,
Everything about you;
You are perfection personified,
From peachy skin and cheeky grin
To the dinky little dimple on your chin,
You're the apple of your mummy's eye,
And that is a fact, that no-one could deny.
Before you came, there were no fun and games
But now that's all changed, thanks to you baby James.

Camilla Hawkins

Baby Boy

Your baby boy is yours to hold
The moments you most treasure
The time will very quickly pass
Your precious times together
And when he's grown and gone away
Your memories will recall the day
You held him close so warm and tender
And when alone you will remember
Those happy times so long ago
These feelings stay and never go.

Hazel Miller

The Mayoress At The Sheltered Workshop

She sat so proudly as we went to see her work,
That child of extra chromosome.
She smiled, revealing wide-spaced, caried teeth,
And tongue, forever darting out and in.
Dispensing spittle on her chin.

She laughed out loudly as we bent to see her work
That child of extra chromosome.
Slant-eyed, round-faced, with thickened herpes lips,
And hair, though short and scurfy, fine and thin,
A friend had tied a ribbon in.

She showed us shyly, the efforts of her work,
That child of extra chromosome.
We looked on fifteen minutes concentration,
The hem, displayed the solitary pin,
Which she, with care, had fastened in.

We left there humbly, the place in which she worked.
That child of extra chromosome.
And in her hands she held my floral spray
For none, I think, would disagree,
That she deserved them more than me.

Doreen Mundy

Ready! Steady! Go!

Ready! Steady! Go!
The starting gun goes bang!
The children are off
Unfortunately, the kids with asthma cough
Ready! Steady! Go!

Ready! Steady! Go!
The wheelchairs zoom down the track
Unfortunately, they have to come back
Ready! Steady! Go!

Ready! Steady! Go!
The wheelbarrow race
At a reasonable pace
Ready! Steady! Go!

Ready! Steady! Go!
All together, people push
They all go whoosh
At the finish line
In no time.

Michael Bate (9)

THREE LITTLE MICES

This is a story of three little mices,
When looking for food came upon dangerous devices,
To catch and trap the three little mices,
'That's not very nice!' said the three little mices.

'We must talk to the lady,' said the three little mices,
The lady turned white to hear the three little mices,
Say . . . 'Leave us alone, we are but three little mices,'
That they wanted no more traps and dangerous devices.

'Very well! But no more than you three little mices,
You must leave alone my chocolates and my ices.
I shall take away the traps and dangerous devices,
And leave a piece of cheese for you three little mices.'

'Agreed, agreed, agreed!' said the three little mices,
'We shall no longer eat your chocolates or your ices.'
So they all lived together, the lady and the three little mices,
Happily ever after . . .
Isn't that nice?

Brian Forsythe

I Want My Mummy Back!

Who is that sitting
Where I used to be?
Getting hugs and kisses
Sat on my mummy's knee.

I used to be her darling
Until baby came along.
Now I'm just a little horror
And everything I do is wrong!

Helen Darlington

UNTITLED

Tree oh tree standing tall
Your mighty secrets to unfold
The moon is high
Clouds draw back
The stars pop out to say hello
Birds asleep, the night is still
- yet there is movement,
I stand and gaze
Eyes wide open in disbelief
The tiny folk gather near my feet
Heart pounding, excitement at this sight
Dare I move - not even a breath
Dancing and playing into the night
They swing on branches
And jump from leaves
I know not where they come from?
Oh mighty tree standing tall
Share your secret, I'll not tell
You shake your branches and stoop . . .
'By magic you have seen this night
My secret of the night unfold
And you to keep this secret whole
That you might return some other night
Go now young friend and leave us be
For we will play while you must sleep
Our worlds do cross but for a moment.'

Barbara Ann Fields

FATHER CHRISTMAS

At the North Pole where it's very cold
Lives a man, who is very old
He lives in a log cabin, and he makes toys
To take at Christmas, to good girls and boys

He has white hair and beard, and wears clothes of red
On Christmas Eve, he delivers toys, to good children in bed
He flies through the air, in a special magical sleigh
Pulled by his reindeers, who like to eat hay

On flies Father Christmas, all through the night
All over the world, what a beautiful sight
When he gets home, his reindeer can rest or play
And all the children have their presents on Christmas Day

C Metcalfe

CHRISTMAS

The season of holly and mistletoe
Again will soon be here,
When our thoughts are occupied
With those that we hold dear

Letters, cards and calendars
Swell the morning post,
Mince pies are a-making
And a turkey on the roast.

Tinsel, streamers, fairy lights
Begin to reappear,
Choristers with muffled ears
Sing so sweet and clear.

Excitement builds inside each child
Imagination has no rein,
Waiting for that Christmas morn,
Oh, to be six again!

Robert E Fraser

Dragon

(Poem written when six)

I know a little dragon
Her name is Caroline.
Strangely every year
She says her age is nine.

One day she visited a castle
And had a bit of hassle.
The knight thought she was dead
She woke up and killed the knight instead.

She now gets lots of mail
Because she's rather ill
'Cos in the fight she lost her tail
And as for the knight, Sir Bill
He wasn't left for dead
The dragon cut off his head
And used it as a *trophy* instead.

Timothy Old (8)

The Great Whale

There once was a whale
called Abigale.
She lives in the seas
with all her beauties.

Her favourite dish
is plenty of fish.
She bites and she eats
with plenty of treats.

Elisha Cole (8)

Don't Want To Go To Play School!

Don't want to go to play school,
Don't want to leave my mum.
My sister's going to the shops,
Oh, please Mum, can I come?
Don't want to play with others,
Don't want to have my snack.
The big school is my brother's,
We pass it on the track.
Get to the gate, I run and hide
Mum says it's all a show.
My teacher opens our door wide,
Bye Mum! It's time to go!

Nicole Brooks

Animals

Animals are everywhere,
in the park, and in the air.
You can find them in the zoo,
and they're in the jungle too.
Animals are very wild
some just like to be with a child.

Neil Bowden (6)

Uncle Fred And Aunty Mary

(For Katie and Ellie)

Uncle Fred and Aunty Mary,
Had the most beautiful, yellow canary.

They loved the canary with all their might,
They even tucked it in at night.

One day, when he got out of bed,
Uncle Fred, found the bird was dead.

He looked at the bird, and his heart filled with dread.
He put his hands up to his head.

'Oh no!' he said, 'the bird is deceased,
I'll have to do something, before it is missed.'

He thought about giving the kiss of life,
And he thought about breaking the news to his wife.

Uncle Fred wondered, about what he could do,
'I'll have to replace it, and quickly too.'

He ran to the pet shop to buy a canary,
Much better than breaking the news to Mary.

He placed the new dicky bird into the cage,
And he got some breakfast from the fridge.

He chuckled at the morning's caper,
And sat down, with his daily paper.

Just then, Aunty Mary got out of bed.
'Fred! Fred! come quick!' she said.

'A miracle has happened!

Last night before I went to bed,
I could have sworn this bird was *dead!'*

Carolyn Bland

Homeless

I wander each street,
Looking for something to eat.
'Tis a very rare treat,
For me to have meat.

I rummage through the tins,
As I hunt in each bin.
I hunt out your scraps,
Moving old mats.

I'm homeless,
Jobless
Moneyless
I rummage in bins,
To keep myself alive.

Ruth Ligget

AND GOD CREATED

God created land and sea,
Grassy hill and wave-washed beach.
God created bird and bee,
Soft worm, shelled snail and wriggly leech.

God created plant and tree
And him and her and you and me
And fruits in summer and flowers in spring
And hot and cold and rain and sun and everything.

Frederick Poole

THANK YOU

Dear Lord,

Thank you that I'm here tonight,
Among the stars that shine so bright,
I thank you I have food and water,
I thank you I have warmth and shelter,
Please bless the refugees, big and small,
Bless them each and bless them all,
I beg you Lord we live in peace,
I beg you that the wars will cease.

Amen.

Samantha Tritton (10)

Tea With Gran

Would you like to come to tea, have chocolate cake, just you and me?
I could read a story, while you finish off your juice
And you could play at Mother and serve up strawberry mousse.

Then after tea, all dishes done,
We could have a little fun,
With paper 'cuts-out' and some 'chalk' we may have time left for a walk.

More stories I could tell you, as we walked along our way,
About the times when I was young, and the games we used to play.

Then back at home with your milkshake
We'll plan a day to make a cake,
Just you and me, again for tea
How delightful that would be.

J Lamble

Spirit Of Hope

Hope. That saviour word -
And word of promise too.
How would life be if that small light
Were not to gleam within the soul?
That flickering, yet persistent, spark
Which simply will not yield -
No matter how the winds of disappointment blow.
For that tiny, glowing, ember deep inside
Can fan a flame so strong
As will defeat and rout the enemy, despair.
Hope ever holds the promise of tomorrow,
When we can look anew,
And rise above the nadir of today.
So, then, embrace that hope with courage,
For - with faith its sure foundation,
And love its cloak -
Hope is the spirit
Which does, God willing, stir the heart,
Confounds the gloom,
And leads us forward with resolve reborn.

Angus W MacDonald

For Peace On Earth

Let peace return tomorrow -
To set the whole world free,
Releasing all from fear and pain,
With your promised destiny.

Lighten again the darkness -
So all can understand,
Why - salvation's 'plough' is turned,
And guided by your hands.

For on a Christmas morning -
So many years ago,
A gift was given to the world -
So *peace* and *love* would grow.

Malcolm Wilson Bucknall

Dog

Four spindly legs, a waggy tail
Ears always so alert.
Hairs all over furniture,
Paw prints etched in dirt.

The very mention of a bath
Sends you off in a huff,
You're always ready for your food,
Oh how you love that stuff!

When we go out for a walk,
It's you that's taking me!
I'm dragged along, we have to stop
At every post, and tree.

Each one must be sniffed around,
And given your attention,
What comes next - what doggies do,
I'm sure I need not mention!

The times when I must leave you,
You show me your displeasure,
But though you make me mad at times,
You're still my greatest treasure!

D Morgan

The Yet To Be

You will travel down roads I will never follow,
You will visit places I will never see.
Wonders you will behold I cannot contemplate,
Many years forward in the yet to be.

I will not be there with you
To comfort and to hold.
Keep your faith in Jesus
Although I'm distant and cold.

Remember the laughter and the fun,
The good times when the journey had just begun;
When friends were many and time was slow.
Live on for me in the future I will never know.

W McMillen

THE BEGINNING OF TIME

So God began His work to do to set all things in order
And to the sea that He had formed He said, 'Don't go beyond
your border,'
Then all that God had made that day He saw and said ''Twas good'
For every living thing He formed, the Earth would bring forth food.

He made the beasts, the fish that swim, the birds that sing and fly
He made the sun for heat and light, the moon for night, the stars on high
In chapter one verse twenty-six these words our God did say
(Gen Ch 1 V26)
'Let us make man in our image; let us make man today.'

So from the Earth God took some clay and formed it to His plan
Breathed into it the breath of life so that was the world's first man.
So the story of creation was now complete, you see.
God saw that all He made was good and we must all agree.

Many thousand years have rolled along since those early days
All that God had promised, the laws of nature still obeys,
The sun his daily course does keep, the moon and stars too
And we the creatures of His hands, His will we try to do.

God made a lovely garden and placed two folks therein
To dress it and keep it, and keep themselves from sin
There was one tree in the garden; forbidden was its fruit
But that was the fruit they wanted, and then of it partook.

'But the day you eat thereof' God said, 'you'll surely die,'
That fruit it sure looked sweet and pleasing to the eye.
The serpent he was hidden, just then he did draw nigh
And told them they could eat the fruit, and would not surely die.

Two thousand years ago God sent His Son to redeem the world
from sin,
All who had their trust in Him, to heaven He'd take them in
And there to be with Jesus and never more depart
From the one who shed His precious blood and loved with all His heart.

The start of the third millennium is drawing very near
It's God alone who knows who will then be here.

Tom Lucas

PLEASE DO YOUR SHARE

Please do your share and make the world a better place to live,
For no-one else can play your part on that stage your God did give.
So, if a chance does come your way and few stand back of you,
Please don't be mute and have your say and speak what's just and true.
Do speak against what's false and sham, attack their varnished lies,
And never hesitate to down their deception and disguise.
Always help your neighbour in his time of strife and stress,
Help him to keep on and win as each one needs success.

Now folks do not be jealous when others do attain,
To that treasure that you or me would not or could not gain.
For various kinds of folk there are upon our worldly sphere,
Some hook their hopes unto a star and do hook them here.
So let us all do what we can and make the path more smooth,
To ease the struggling race for man who's borne so much abuse.

James O'Kane